D0779453

SLIDE TO UNLOCK

Slide to Unlock
Copyright © 2020 by Julie E. Bloemeke

Cover image by Julie E. Bloemeke

Cover design by Seth Pennington

Author photograph by M

All rights reserved. No part of this book may be reproduced or republished without written consent from the publisher, except by reviewers who may quote brief excerpts in connection with a review in a newspaper, magazine, or electronic publication; nor may any part of this book be reproduced, stored in a retrieval system, or transmitted in any form, or by any means be recorded without written consent of the publisher.

Sibling Rivalry Press, LLC
PO Box 26147
Little Rock, AR 72221

info@siblingrivalrypress.com

www.siblingrivalrypress.com

ISBN: 978-1-943977-76-5

Library of Congress Control No.: 2019953148

By special invitation, this title is housed in the Rare Book and Special Collections Vault of the Library of Congress.

First Sibling Rivalry Press Edition, March 2020

SLIDE TO UNLOCK

Julie E. Bloemeke

SIBLING RIVALRY PRESS
DISTURB/ENRAPTURE
LITTLE ROCK, ARKANSAS

for anyone left on hold

Dialing In

Call Waiting

On the Line

Cellular

We'd like to say how things are, perhaps because we hope that's how they might actually be. We attempt to name, identify, and define the most mysterious of matters: sex, love, marriage, monogamy, infidelity, death, loss, grief. We want these things to have an order, an internal logic, and we also want them to be connected to one another.

— Cheryl Strayed

Writing letters is actually an intercourse with ghosts and by no means just with the ghost of the addressee but also with one's own ghost…One can think about someone far away and one can hold onto someone nearby; everything else is beyond human power…after the postal system the ghosts invented the telegraph, the telephone, the wireless. They will not starve, but we will perish.

— Franz Kafka

…and that cellular will be the death of us, I swear, I swear…

— Never Shout Never

DIALING IN

SLIDE TO UNLOCK

after the iPhone entry screen, 2007—2016

Caught in the present tense,
we are continuously poised

to receive its three-word
command, the insistence

we open with a fall:
Slide.

Involuntary,
we unknowingly slip

into habit, press
our print from left

to right, unaware
of what uninvited

light will bow our heads.
When this trinity opens

our bodies, we respond
with our curious hands.

We no longer read the words.
A call expects an answer, a dark

screen, a touch. We are undone
by the promise of resolution,

temptation. Once, we could depend
on the corded spiral of miles,

delay ourselves with the orbit
of finger wheel, change

15

the exchange with a switch
hook. We could even leave

the rotary to ring, unheard
in the absence. Then, we

housed it for distance,
carving an alcove

into the wall.
Hold the line, we said.

Now, we are keyed constant,
pocketing names, waking

to flashes, feeling through the dark
before we open our eyes,

our cells carrying
the call of possible.

There is no signal
to prepare us

for the arrival
of that unresolved name,

its bright trick of letters.
It arrives after decades of silence,

the demand for an answer
so pressing it stings a vibration,

its invisible stigmata left
in our unsuspecting palms,

an irrevocable consequence
of reach out and touch someone.

THE HANG UP

after Bird Lake, Michigan

I

Bared together, our feet touch
under lake shallows.

We hold each other
from the inevitable.

The last time.

You made me promise to be silent.
I made you promise to meet here,

our bodies back to water, place
where we began.

Part of me has already left.
Neither of us can stay.

There is a plane, ticketed,
your name already on a seat.

There is a letter, signed.
It says I am theirs.

Geography has done
our dirty work.

II

Us: how we believed
in romantic endings,

the cinema swell
of happiness. And now.

We cannot even allow
the words, the tongues

that could keep us.
It's true: if I heard your voice

I would follow it.
And still, I break it all.

The blue paper,
a gift from you.

Written words,
my pocket to yours.

A potential breach
of our promise.

You take my face
in your hands.

The longer we hold
the more there is.

The salt of our bodies,
our press into each other,

the sweat and slip,
the tears and wet,

as you shake against
my skin, as I buckle

into yours. We are loud
against the past, the way

we sunned ourselves
in love's heat

on the dock, now
pointing beyond us.

How we hold
to each other, wanting

to shatter the impossible
onslaught of time,

how we were broken
without knowing

how broken, the griefs
of death and birth

also affixed to our silence.
Seventeen is too young

everyone said.
And they were right.

III

And now the letter,
my betrayal of words,

all the things I wanted
you to remember,

sentences I hoped
might lead you back,

or somewhere, or to peace.
I waited for your anger,

but all that came
was the shaking

of your body.
You were not used

to unexpected gifts.
We held tighter still,

watching the sun fall,
lashing itself against

the inevitable waves.
Somewhere our parents

are shouting our names
into the night, dialing

the phones, anchored
to the walls of our houses.

They are trying to find us.
But we hold to the lock

of our bodies.
I cannot remember how

we let go.

CALL WAITING

GLASS CITY

returning to Toledo, seventeen years later

To assemble a land,
polish it to sea.

The escape of altered
things. The branches

that follow. Weave
a terrain, parison

in clumsy hands. Learn
to write from refraction.

Add windows, fragile
in their divided ways.

Don't miss that they corner,
prefer the word pane.

Take the beaker of trees,
the liquid of what loves.

Imagine ponds of glass:
an electric so fragile

it breaks to the touch.
Don't assume

the name, proclaim
it holy. This is the city

where bones anneal,
where letters glow sand

cells into the body.
Under this rock, another.

Beneath this cobalt, a wing.
Here everything is molten,

kissed, meant to be spun,
the shape of it blown

into being. See how we chase
memory, distortion,

even as it shatters in our hands?
Look: when I hold it all

the sun burns every reflection,
fires it back to new.

Is it any wonder then
I will call on the I, the you,

our past, this city,
word them into glass too?

FINGER SEQUENCE IN BLUE

after Canon, Georgia

In this story, the train.
Or, a broken vial in the trestle.
The ground responds, emphatic:
vibration before the beam.

In this story, the train.
The problem with love?
It is love. A harness for perception.
I used a you. You used a me too.

Still they plume me back, these refrains.
Back to where? Within. There.
That water day of   *no   good   bye*,
our signed decades of silence.
My blue note still sears,
scars your pocket.

Think of all those waves
that cracked the shore without us.
No. It is too early in the story.
We haven't gotten to Paris, yet.
That too will come.

But I am not thinking of Paris.
Only this sudden heaviness
over my hip, burning deeper
into the seam. What? Another letter?

No, the I that claims itself,
a first-person phone, the taunt of key/
stroke, pass/code, voice/
mail, our answering/machine,

the easy blue of a speech balloon
marked *delivered*.
In this story,

how long do we wait?

Talon the whistle, unsidle
the bolt. Already the horizon
shivers with blindness,
electric in my oncoming ear.

SCAR SEASON

As a girl I wanted one, simple,
uninterrupted, those zags
of tell and hide: injury, surgery,
the open and closed mouth
of them all at once.

After my friend fell from her bike,
she had lines tied into her chin,
little shocks of thread that poked
their spikes when I touched them.

I did not think about the blood,
the needles, how she wailed
at the split, how my hands covered
the gap as I stumbled her home.

All I saw was the glare of accident
on her skin, the remarkable way
they fixed her, how her face stayed
together when she smiled, screamed.

I told no one why I raced my Schwinn
down Dead Man's Hill, why I jumped
from the dare tree, rollerskated into the ravine.

I grew lonely over the bruises and scrapes,
the adornments that healed and disappeared,
the betrayal of Band-Aids.

Then: chicken pox. The threat of my body
tied to itch, my mother photographing
my marked back, stunned
at the terrific colonies of red.

Don't, everyone said, when I touched
them. *You will scar*. And I thought

of the bike, the falls, the skates sitting
barren. And all I had to do was release,

lift the scab each time it formed until finally,
on my ankle, a round crater,
a universe to claim: the scar without

the accident, the mark without the wound,
how I was simply given
what I tried so hard to create.

BLOOD

At eight I am left,
my first night
alone in the house.

I watch the thin threads
of blood join down
the textured wall.

It is a braille I cannot read.
I know only that it is up to me.
I find water, soap. The red goes

pink, even brown, with the pass
of my Cinderella washcloth, her face
marred by rust. I cry to no one,

my brother dashed off for stitches.
I am not sure why I am here,
know only to do what I am told.

There will be three between
his brows, a third eye that sees.
I cannot know this yet.

I work to the floor: the marks of him,
the failure of water. How do I lift this?
How can I wash it away?

I smell iron and Ivory, feel how simply
our bodies break, rub away what minutes
before ran through him, secret,

as he was laughing, twirling,
before the stumble, split.
I have no idea

how I cleaned it all,
but when they came home, stained
gauze still in my mother's hand,

I waited for her to tell me
how the floor sparkled
so bright we could eat off of it.

As if this would be comfort, or love,
as if her silence wasn't the meal
I devoured, hungry to be whole.

LETTERS ON THE AIR (I FEEL LOVE)

after Donna Summer

try me   fill me

I know I know I know I know

      that green lamp   swag spin   sunken

          living room   pillar votive

          burning, burning to   *don't touch.*

shadows. he sits. orange pinpoint flare. darkness.

            smokecurl smell.

I stand on the coffee table.

      he does not stop me

            with language.

I break every rule   I break every

            line

      I jump.

he talks. not to say *no*. not to say *yes*.

      to say: *listen*   to ask:

what is really left in the rain?

      I say the cake.

      I say her umbrella. *no.*

I say, mid-spin: *her heart?*

ice clink in the drink. *think*, he says.

think.

I see her yellow dress

      I hear her run for a man she loves.

I don't know longing.

      I don't know yes.

but she is running

      and I

            climb

               jump

the lid rattles on the glass jar

      I jump

         I spin

    I spin to fall

I get up

      thick shift of room

the flexing light

my shadows on the wall a disco

I feel love   *I feel love*

     this   flare   spin

       I'm bad   *I'm so so bad*

the imagined man in the chair: *think:*

     another word for *muse*

     this voice that makes me

   it's so good   *it's so good*

and already this young I am bad

      bad because I want

because even though I do not know

     I know

I can   I will

     I will make this song

       mine   at seventeen

I will have my question too

I will take this body

     and torment it

      with memory, regret.

I will be so so bad in how I want

me who has the cake, the rain, the yellow dress,

        the man to run for, the letter from the overcoat.

why isn't it enough?

        come on baby, dance that dance.

        I fall down.

I am the cake, the rain, the recipe in your hands

        your hands, these

            letters   on

              the air

DARKROOM

Even at ten he was saying,
sneak with me in the dark
room, that under place
of his house that smelled
of chemical and brine, home
to amber bottle, metal reels,
words like fixer, stop bath, developer.

Standing before the door,
I could feel the cool spiral
of wrong turning through
the dirt of me, the fang
of want and wait, shifting
under the tines of my ribs.

I wanted to see and not,
I wanted to show and not.

In that black room, with
only a film of sunlight,
he stood under the dark
of light-tight boxes, went
to unbutton his pants,
looking to me, the door,

saying, suddenly very fast,
Come on, now you show me

and I ran out, letting light in,
jumped into the beanbags
in his basement, hid my face
deep in their velvet, wanting
to merge into their colors,
all that burning: red, ochre,
an orange too close to fire.

I could hear him watching
me—his breath, now a small laugh.
He said it again, closer now.
Come on, I won't tell.

And I turned my head to him,
covered my face with the convenient
afghan, wanting to remember my
world, his, before the holes.

He flopped down beside me, his whisper
broken. Now he pinched my arm,
said *Race ya*! and fled upstairs,
banging the screen door.

Outside: the place where we could
scrape our knees to blood on the bark
of trees, dangle effortlessly upside down,
our shirts riding up, exposing our stomachs,

where for awhile we could still see
that world before, knowing at any moment
we had legs to run. But, on this heavy
branch, I swayed, this time holding
my shirt, knowing that under my clothes

was something that made boys whisper,
made them convince me
to hidden places, rooms
with dust traveling in narrowed apertures,

where eyes fixed, where I was spiraling
toward and running from, hiding then escaping,
full tilt and full stop, knowing somehow

that for me to take off what I'd put on
would be to close the shutter
on a photograph I could never undo.

FOREIGN EXCHANGE

He led me up the stairs,
my unsure hand in his,
Z, from Peru, who seemed
overwhelmed by all of it: my drunk
older brother, our English, this forbidden
high school Christmas party.

I was thirteen, on my second fuzzy navel,
sweet peach and orange swirled
in a plastic cup. I sat on the edge
of the bed, feigned sophistication,
pretended in my staggering Spanish:
Guapo. Beso. Muy bueno.

He sat down beside me, held
my hand, asked me, broken,
*Rubia, I think your heart
is oro, like this?* touching
my blonde hair just barely.

I wanted anything to happen
in his accent, his jagged unknown
words, the soft way he looked at me
so unlike American boys. I leaned
closer and he stood, searching
the bookshelf. I asked him how to say
orange and *peach* and *drunk*, laughing.

He found a book, opened it, pointed
to Peru, his mountains, the blurs
of green and ruins, guiding my hands
over this landscape, his home.
As he talked, I felt my head spin,
his hand on my back to steady me.

He set down my cup, showing me coffee trees,

Corpus Christi costumes, the totora boats
drying upward to the sky, the salt collectors
in the Sacred Valley, sand. I felt the clock
of the room wind tight against me, remembered
how to say *Tengo fiebre, no,*

¿Tengo hambre?, no, ¿Tengo enferma?
Estas enferma? He asked so close
and sensing, lifted me from
the bed, got me to the bathroom,
rubbed my back, held my hair.

The word for peach: *melocotón.*
The word for orange: *naranja.*
The word for drunk idiot: *You*
must not call yourself that.

How I leaned against him, the truth:

Everything has happen and nothing
has happen, mi rubia.

And that too, was something.
Perhaps it was everything.

STATUE PRAYER AT FIFTEEN

Mother, in my world,
virginity is defined
by loss.

Admission: an easy
litmus. As soon as I open
to confession, their touches
turn from want to sister.

But here I am on my knees, still
in this jaded light, your static mouth
jeweled in the cut of votive flame.

What if I believe this
is my way? That for once
I have found the diadem of *no*
as a kind of salvation, at last

a place where I am heard?
What if I think of your face
smiling in *yes*? When I whisper
in the thresh of desire, what if I pray
to hold, wait for the one true found?

I cannot bear their eager lips,
their breath heavy at the chapel
of want, the way they try their hands
at the altar of my legs. I soften
to their kisses, yes, the rare
sweetness of their words when
they are without motive.

Someone has painted a heart
on your hand. Someone has
touched you with gold. I tip
my forehead to your cracked hem,

hardened in its line. My knees grow numb
with leaning. I whisper up to you:

Oh Mary. Oh marry. Oh merry.
Is it all a trinity of trickery, a prayer
of persuasion, of false faith?

And still the problem
of this star, crossed
over my body, forever
this burden we call light.

BODIES OF WATER: DISCOVERING
CÔTE D'AZUR ON BIRD LAKE

after Claude Monet's Antibes Seen from La Salis, *Toledo Museum of Art*

I

In the swirl of teenage years,
there is a call beyond

tailgates and bowling alleys,
beyond pizza and the labyrinth

of shopping malls, of hiding
in the basement to crank

the music forbidden.
There is the lure

of the *town turned gold*
by the sun, the one stone square

where she stands, brings
Monet's *Antibes* into her body.

It is here she admits
the letters she's written

to herself, the cursive that contains
why and *God* and every last

one   lone   lonely   alone
the singular strokes on the paper,

how they angle for arms, need
the press of letters, the ache

away from solitude.
She thinks of the violence

of one pen pushed into paper,
period, the needle through

the firmament of pulp, the dot
that ends the sentence, the brush

that lets the light. This, her
way to see the stars.

This, her way to avenge
an eclipse. And the sudden

knowing that the hand
is more than itself.

II

She leaves. The world flicks
by in fast motion, maybe weeks,

maybe hours, until he arrives,
the boy who unknowingly stands

on the same stone square, his feet
in parallel over the once-print of hers.

Behind him, Hughes' *Ophelia*,
her eyes an invitation to *no*

before her drowned *yes*.
But France is another country.

Another story. In the aureate blues,
he travels, transports, fathoms

Monet's hand, holding the boar bristle
stained with pigment, oil, broken

color, between his fingers the dot
to impasto, feathering to city,

the gold of another shore.
And they come then, the letters

he's written alone, the journal
in his pocket scratched

with *why* and *God* and every last
one   lone   lonely   alone

He insists his mind is stippled,
warped, claims *no one sees the city*

I see. But now the waves,
an olive branch,

and the one question:
Is the hand in his only his?

III

Press together the cover
of front to back, begin to end.

Only the text block
separates them.

They arrive to bodies, raised
from the page, outside

the border, that shared
stone square. And here,

on Bird Lake, en plein air,
she is saying, *you stood there too,*

I felt you. And they understand now,
the hand, the words, the sudden

skip through the cage of bone,
the dried petals now veined with light.

On this dock, leading to water,
to unknown, there is sunset, then night,

the flash of the mariner's green
before the moon harnesses the sky.

There's the ages, seventeen, there's
these new words yet to be written:

the *once* and *open* and *time*, unspined
in their mouths: to greet, seal, transform,

to open, breathe, mouth to mouth,
to give, receive, this first kiss.

SEVENTEEN

But then there was the boy
who shared communion with me,
held my hands in prayer,
who kissed me as I told him — virgin —
and responded:

*Why do we think
there's only one way?*

And in this he let love. I broke,
lit myself to him, at last seen whole,
my body no longer divided into bases.

And tonight, over the water,
the moon piercing the prow
like an answered question,
we spread ourselves naked,
face the stars. He traces my body

with his hands, as if to create
me, takes joy in seeing the light
empty over me, our want without
end. He says: *receive, just receive*

and I think of the cup, shared
as he passes his shaking fingertips
over the delve between my hips
as he meets them with his lips,
as his face sets between
my legs. I open the wings

of my knees for him, he divides
me with his tongue. His first
taste and mine, here under the clouds
that unseam their needles of darkness.

In this first, I want another, for him
to receive me as I come, for my first
tandem open to be for his mouth,
because of his mouth, to echo
from my body and into his,

so when he misses this, us, the newness
of it all, he can remember his name
called from the pleasure of my throat,
he can remember *yes* and *God*.

YOU'RE BREAKING UP

The last time I saw you
we were almost naked
and breaking up though
could we have known either, then?

Only the phone with its curls
and nonface would give us enough
courage to say to a mouthpiece: *it's over*.
And even then you would hold

the line, say *Wait. Please*. And I could hear
you getting high, wanting to ease out
and hang on. And how I would keep

us too, talking us back
into that room where again,
I had been trying on you
to get over him. That blue
room with its corduroy walls,

where we were slipping and playing
Todd Rundgren and you were whispering —
maybe begging —*think of me* —as your hand
made its way down my hips to my thighs

and how, for just this once, I would lie
back for you, even when you knew
I would never let you in. And how we shared

beer from a dark bottle, and how later
I took you close enough that you began
to sing, even after Todd had long given up:
seeing you, seeing you.

And after, how we faced the ceiling,
hanging the possibility of sex

like paper stars, glittering
and just out of reach.

And how neither of us ever hung up,
falling asleep over the wires, waking
in the morning, the receiver somehow still
and dead on the pillow next to each of us.

TELEPHONE, CALL

after The Great Gatsby

That *shrill metallic urgency*, now
the persistent buzz, the toggled

jackhammer of bees in a pocket, under
a skirt. Don't miss the nearness

of hip, or groin, all of our green lights
zipped in, or not. How we reach over

water, the longing hands, the hope
that reflects through mist and myth:

time and past, the elusive we created.
Then: lover's shouts shot over wires,

the curlicue cord, the voice brought
on a silver plate to interrupt

other voices: insistence, the thorn
of desperation, the mouth

piece wanting everyone held
in distraction, revelation.

Now, in our hands, no one to block
us, to say *Excuse me* or *I'm afraid*

he can't take your call, our fingers
do the walking, texting, and we press

to each other in voice, send, the naked
pictures that keep us in sweat, follow

the green light beckoning, the pulse
of betrayal. See now how we persist:

standing, charged, docked,
left in the ring of desire.

TOUCH TONE: RANDOM ACCESS MEMORY

4: the former first, soundpress, to get to you

Rattle and Hum, seventeenth track

7: follows in the line

Antibes Seen From La Salis, silent in its frame

5: completes the right angle

My blue note kept/in your pocket

6: takes the dash

Shutter open, clicking in/the way I look back through you.

3: brings us higher

Trinity, Mary, virginity.

1: as farthest point. Don't say left.

Our hands/Venice from water/Paris, pair is, pair us,

0: say center, as lowest, empty to ring

Piction blue/together we are sealed under.

No. Answer.

Once, twice. Switch hook.

The way we never remember leaving.

THE CALL

My husband never left me
hanging,
a man
of his word.

No wait
game, no elaborate
lie, no benefit of doubt
dance. None. Not even
a question. If he said it was,

it was. Steel truths:
I will be there at three.
I will call at nine.

Like clockwork, like gold
band, like *Of course*
it was never another way,
was it? he says,

with others, did they leave
you to wait? Cause you to doubt?
This is a language I don't know,
and one you shouldn't either,
touching me

bare. And this is why the others
left him, maybe, his shining
dependability too easy.

He kisses me for each call you never
made, he tongues my spine, presses
me to the place I can breathe, says
Trust is not a line, not a bauble, not
a big mouth open, exposure.

When he says the word, the word
is the word. The word isn't only love,
it is my collapse into this bed
that folds me in its mouth,

never leaves my faulty wires
frayed with hope, disconnected,
ringing, ringing in the blank
and forgotten dark.

SEEING AN EX ON THE BEACH

I saw you walking on the beach.

I thought

I saw you   walking
          on the beach.

Body:
response before   click
brain   before
words.

Imagine that space:
perception   before
the realized.

Hover there: stay in that
moment before
the plug of one   meets
the other.

Observe the body: feel
how it is: as when   caught
in a lie.   Terror   relief
mimic each other.

The straight flush:
toe to pricked-aware scalp
winding back down to knee give
and back through again, and maybe
again, again

until the brain can note the details
that lied   him into being:

the gait, yes

the jet hair, yes
the sunglasses we bought together, yes.

The greyhounds: strange, but maybe.
The nose, no. Unless the trick of light? No.

The familiar body lines
in the unfamiliar grid: confirmation.

Body, still pumping in its current
relief, devastation.

Saying: go
saying: hide
saying: run, embrace
saying: sift into sand, disappear.

You: stranger, man I loved
for a fierce not-even-second

walk
no awareness at all

as you lift your face, smile,
pass the electric
me

and the dogs follow: nip
then bite   the empty   air

after you.

OBSERVATIONS FROM THE BASE

after Lake Santeetlah, North Carolina

The problem with heights:
They are heights.

Again the resistance
of water.

How each kiss, somehow,
is an attempt to recreate,
not make new.

Lust: a four-letter word.
Also: what.

I have self-covenants:
One: to imagine no
other when with you.

By the fire, I slip.
I curse myself
for not loving better.

When I ask you if I am
someone else you say,
Only you.

I want to be this mountain.
But then I swim.

The problem with covenants:
They are covenants.

Later you say this to me:
The blank space is how
I honor it, deliciously gone.

Even the fog makes promises,
spans the hips of mountains.

Such great heights.
The fire wet ashes
we cannot light again.

SEVERED

after Frida Kahlo's Self-Portrait with Cropped Hair

Suited, I become (un)dressed.
Heft of steel at my neck,
nest of snakes at my feet.

No mantilla, no rebozo,
my broken hospital gown
hanging over *Gringolandia*.

I am no fair dove in this
pinstriped elephant, my
brow bones deceiving.

I raise what is sharp.
I take my hair down.

All that flowers turns
to threads, rising up
against the fabric of you.

See the blood shirt,
the barren lapel. Only
my shoes remain, point

back to the sinister chair,
the true pocket of this coat:
scissors, paintbrush,

the fire work of my heart,
stilettos turned inward
past every last rib.

COMPOSITION

The letter is already bandaged,
cuts and pastes of phrases, plasters
of characters, greenstick words, broken
to mend. Still delete, still return,
sometimes only the repeating eye
of the ellipsis. The words we can
never bring to key. What message
after the refrain of silence?

What to say to the way we lost
each other, locked in that not
wanting to go forward and still wanting
one another? Then: it was the young
necessity of leaving. How we fixed
a self to that point, everything
appearing to move. Only we anchor
us back, insist all is progress.
Time: the concrete zephyr.

There is no punctuation
for the nightmares, how I reach
for him in sleep, or how he passes
his index finger in repeated regret
wearing the watchband to thin.
My gift. As if to rub out time.
As if, by touch, to stop it.

Is there a comma that bears
the years, a period that will rise
as monument to the inked
puncture of absence?

How I whisper letters to him
in the cover of night, how his mouth
returns my name in prayer. The flagrance
of exclamation points, the parentheses

that strain to raise their locks
after seventeen years.

Maybe we justify the text.

Maybe only the question
marks.

BLACK PLACE

after Georgia O'Keeffe's Black Place I

Right side, third dip up, there is a hair.
Hers? The brush? I wish it were mine,
the silk way she merges these greys

to greyer still. How moored I am
in the ruffled campus of myself,
stagnant as these villi. Tell me

I can hear it better now.
The yielding folds call
out, say *yes, yes, you do have wounds*.

They are my ever landscape,
these two knuckled hills.

Forget attempts at purple, green,
even a pristine anything.

Take only that cut of night, that twist
and drop that says no, not this,

not here, not ever again.

ON THE LINE

PULSE STORM, 2008

Windows open, crack
of Georgia thunderstorm, rain-dense
needles dropping, and us:

curled to naked in this heavy bed.
Your hand rests on the cleave
at the base of my spine, your home
place on my body. How you have loved
me in my ugliness, which could be beauty.

And still you see more, turn
me to the chapters of light, how
you claim I turn you too. This deep
root: ours. The wound: mine.

Why are we never enough?

Why does the chimera come, wound
as ache, empty knock at my chest,
as one person, taunting me
in my uninhibited half-awake?

What was left undone?

For years I rolled over, woke up,
denied him full entry, but still
the persistence: song on the radio, catch
in my voice, parallels of handwriting

in the mailbox, the scent of eucalyptus
that yanked me to aching girl, to inner
voice, to why. All these years of *no*
are rising in my throat.

And under this storm
I climb within myself
to tell you the truth:

that my brain has begun otherwise,
seeking out the memory of him,
triggering itself, going over and over
the scenes again, burning in want.

I've tried it all: distraction, gin, prayer,
the patient therapists, the meds. I am left
with another possible pearl: contact.

And you turn to me, kiss
my forehead, my lips, take my face
in the cup of your hands
as you have so many times
over our fifteen years together.

You say: *Find him. Write him.*
We will love each other even through.

And then, after we make love,
after the rain stops her rivulets
on the glass, you bring my hand
to my chest, speak further:

Write truth. You are called for this.

And before I can answer:

You think he is the story,
but the book is you.

Neither of us can know what doors
we will unleash, what bodies
of water we will undam.

But now we've invited the lightning.

LOCK BRIDGE, 2008

He stands in the middle, night
Paris rising from the Seine. Rain
parts, leaves a gloss, flecked

catches of light, the seemingly endless
brass, hitched and held, one over the other.
They've begun a new tradition: lock

a lock to the bridge, drop the key
into the river's bed. The weight
of this, already creaking Pont des Arts,

beginning the bow. So many combinations
of *we*, or *us*, sealed in the vow of click,
how each one dialed into the heart, bound

to the tumble, willingly chose the heft
in hand. What of the others, taken
from a pocket, a simple rotary of thumb

and forefinger, turning the secret
code? He lifts them now, one after the other,
notes each as title, story stamped to lock body:

Master, Triumph, Hero, Guard, Honesty,
Fraime, Protex, Valor, Climax, Best.

All this locking as owning, as holding cell,
claiming love. He traces over lovers,
initials, scratched as with nail or key,

as if to free or bind themselves, fingers
gone numb for attempted eternal.
But none of this stops the yearning,

the wondering where our lives
have been these last seventeen years.

In Paris, he feels the collapse,
the insistence upon

insistence, no seeming end to the vanishing
point. These once promises, now small,
cumulative prisons of love — persuasions

to do what cannot be undone. He unlocks
his phone, hovers over me, pin of my city,
distant in the map of his palm.

CELLULAR

VENICE

Us: wood built from water.

Our cells temporary, vibrant,
winding and dividing
one over the other,
one hand in the other
body pressed to body.

We imagine mitosis.

I push my fingers into
you, try to absorb, bring
you inside me, to thrive
in my marrow, divide
your quintessence into,

to take the shining star of you
holding the light of me
making us release
into glorious.

Yes, arch into me,
triumphant, yes, knit
your bones to mine, if only for
now. Let me carry
you in me, make you involuntary.

Do not talk of new life,
of something other we'd become.

No.

I mean, you, a new meiosis, me,
my chambers beating into
yours, all of your soul fire
leaving dust each time I run
my hands through my hair.

Let me carry you everywhere.

My body calls for yours,
envelope, diatom,
us only as one fingerprint
on the sheet of life.

This is not marriage.
This is not two joined as one.
This is me, infusing you,
bearing into, us

oceans away, living apart,
breathing together, our bodies
ringing, going on the ecstasy
of mitochondria, the ribosomes of exchange,

the very relief that there *is*, yes,
one cell pressed to another
with joy, with resolution,
membrane to membrane.

Sunken under Venice, there is
one branch of magnolia soulangeana,
resting her xylem, holding up a city,
suspended from decay, no oxygen
to take in or give out: stasis.

In places there are poplars to oaks, elms
to conifers, but here, in our bodies,
this one place, underneath the shadow
of San Giacomo dell'Orio,
there is us, in overlay

holding up lovers and pigeons,
mongers and gapers, an orange
crushed between the pavers.

It is here we always have been,
silent beneath the chaos, pressed together
for storm, told we are sinking.

We know better.

There is no place but here,
submerged, the flower of me,
the flower of you, both coded to open,
but brought instead to salt,
converted to everlasting.

ELECTRIC MAIL

You chime in, shock
me back from work,

and I am sudden: swift shot,
crown-to-toe electric in you,
ravenous to read.

Your name presses
from pixels, a promise
of no more silence.

I trace your bends and twists,
letters that stand up in your name,
remember the seventeen years

I searched, my fingers curving
over the imprint of your initials,
your spell. And now you rise
over my screen, come back to me.

It would have been too much
to visit with my body, call
with my voice, send my cursive
to your door. But now I can read

your words, arced at last for me,
savor the scatter of your type without
the loops and dips of your written.

I cannot press your stationery
to my face, see the smudges
you erased on the page, breathe
the scent of you lingering
in the lines. I cannot pocket

you, as before, make an altar

of the few things your hands
once made for me.

We have wires to protect
us now. You are an ocean
away. Still we type, touch
without touch, come closer,

arrive more, and I let you in: my car,
my coat, my sheets. I hold you

in my hand, shocking. I tell myself
these are only letters, pushed through
anonymous keys. We have not lifted

a pen, committed to paper. But already
we are in my deepest vacant room. I take
you to the bed I never left. We fall

together, insisting *there is safety
in letters*, as we write more, seal
ourselves furiously into what

we already know.

EMAIL FROM MUSEO CORRER

I

You are in Venice, everywhere the shift
of tide. Some scenes I conjure myself, releasing
my version from its pages. Others you create
for me: the flight of pigeons, their expectant eyes,
an adagio lifting through San Marco. Even the sun
grabs the columns as if to stop itself.

And after this paragraph: sudden space.
You scumble, mention you are wearing sunglasses,
though now it is almost night. That you ordered
a glass of the soave I told you I dreamed
of one day drinking. That you are holding
the screen in your hands, barely
able to read. You tell me you try to type,
but the tears are merciless. At first
I think you say this for the beauty
of Venice. Or because you are walking
the wish. Then I think—selfishly—maybe
it is because of me, or us, though I do not say it.

I am sitting in the pine forest alone
as I read this. Thank God I am.
Two years we have been writing: art, books,
travel: never a mention of our past, of an us,
never a cross into the intimate. But here
in the city of water, bridges, you reveal
the glass truth: the unexpected text
no letter could prepare us for:
Your marriage is over.

The strings in me snap. I buckle
into the needles, all of their spines
breaking against me. How to navigate an ocean?
Because now all I want is to reach you,

to do what I once knew best: to save you
with my body, to steal for a moment
what I should not. But I am left
with a pulsing cursor, a tainted screen,
the need to share when I can only offer:

I write faith, pray that my words
will somehow light any candle
within you. I tell you there is a chapel:
San Giacomo dell'Orio. You promise
to find it. I send, sick with words
that cannot save a thing.

II

As my words depart, yours arrive. Our crossing
in the ether. Another message: *What I did not say*
was why I am telling you this now.
It was the painting. Antibes *is here. Our Monet.*
At first, I cannot make sense, think
you are using metaphor, but no.
The painting—our painting—
is in Venice, on leave from Toledo.

And my hands cover my face and I am back,
further into our younger, unstained selves,
the two of us holding each other before that daubed
precipice, glittering toward the city, to Côte d'Azur,
how we vowed one day we would see it all together.

Neither of us have been to the painting since.
And now, you spell more: it has its own wall
in the Museo Correr. As if waiting for this, or us.

III

It is the questions that open now, the way I press
my fingernails into my palm until I anchor

myself back in. It is the way you type
a word, only to pause and touch the mole
I once vowed myself into, claiming my space
on your body. The place I kissed that last day
before we drowned for seventeen years of silence.

And now you walk the streets, their narrow veins,
bloodless as you move through them. You have
dinner alone, looking to the Rialto as the sun collapses,
as you will me to walk over, without a word,
to give my body as lightning or escape, as anything
that will close the pain.

All of this you can never say, and never will,
out of respect or deference or secret I cannot know.
Instead you hang our landscape in the gallery
of hope, trusting in all that seems to remain.

INFIDELITY

Hear how they come in,
the stories and their players:
at the graveside, after too much
wine, Thanksgiving, in the recesses
of once-forbidden conversation.
Question those tongues of energy:
how he kept his wedding ring
in the glove box, how she slid
the key under the flower pot, but only
on Thursday. I came to our marriage
with flagrant truths, progeny
of ancestors openly in other beds,
ruined vows, the choice sometimes
to break, the choice sometimes to endure.
You asked for my hand, I gave you
my body of story, the slips and sins
that came to making me. What you did
not know then, faithful man,
is that you too came through the secret
broken, the curious myths unraveling
over the years: the locked closet,
the strange hair on the pillow. Further
back we suspect more: conjecture
of muddied lace, the promise that began
as pure but fractured for desire
or misery or because the lost
returned in a kiss that seemed
salvation. We swear and build
on the untold, pass it down as our own
eyes, our bodies. How even now
I have to tell my hands *stay with me*,
fold tight to each other, remain
in prayer under the table's darkness.

SWITCHING OFF AT CEDAR POINT

Years later, after hearing
of your divorce, her infidelity,
I remember another time:

The four of us—my husband,
your wife—would switch
children, hip-jiggle babies

so the other could ride, so we all
could take a turn to throw our hands
to sky and scream legitimately
all the way down.

We did this over and over
laughing ourselves to younger,
such pink spun release.

And well after dark,
just before closing,
in the shuffle of strollers
and lines, you and I are alone
on a crowded shuttle.

Without a word, you rest
your heavy head in my lap,
face away. And whether
from exhaustion or want

I allow myself one last pleasure:
to run my fingers through
the thick question of your hair.

You slide one arm beneath
my knees, the other over the top,
press back to me, as if to keep
from falling. Or screaming.

And when we stopped, they were waiting:
the man, the woman, the sticky sleeping
children, all the beautiful ones
we'd once said yes to.

GOSPEL OF TEXT, BOOKS I-IV

I. Cell Correspondence

I touch you
in the privacy

of my hand.
You slide,

unlock
me in yours.

I have not seen how
you look at me,

our eyes unmet
for decades now.

You even carry me
in your pocket,

the one over
your heart,

the one lower
than your hip.

It is how we build
the membrane,

body ourselves
into each other:

I am your creation.
You are mine.

The walled envelope
of truth: we risk

no
exposure

living in the *sent* cells
of our messages.

II. After Weeks of Silence You Text Me One Photo Without Words

It contains this:

lake	waves	three mountains
clouds	polished sky	two birds
an edge	a shore	crossing

And the outline
of your body
over it all.

It is how you see a landscape:
vast, inevitable.

No it isn't.

It is a photograph
of how you miss me.

III. Text Confession Sans Sphallolalia

It happens
when we take
the memory of us
into present
tense,
when in
real
real?
time
your words appear
as pinpoint selves:

Kiss   touch   taste

and, curious,
I don't say *stop*
I say *please*
I say *oh God*
which can mean
so many ways
I touch
the map
of your name
resting over
my heart
line
these letter
squares
we call keys
and I wait
for the beat
of your dots
small tongued
circles pulsing
in the pause
which means
you are giving

me
more   more
my eyes open
my body charmed
to the press
your sealed thoughts
unzipped
after decades

all of our carefulness
lost
to touch

to text
in my hands
your long-revealed prayer:

you too want

our bodies wired
as one.

IV. Picture from Bed

You text:
Send me?

This means:
Send me a picture.

I am in bed alone. You too.
You want me captured, now
when we are slightly
drunk, able to think of touch.

For once, I do not pause over
the small curve of darkness
under my eyes.

I snap immediately.

I do this
not for the photo
I won't send,

but because
I want to be
the last question

before you fall
asleep

ROTARY ODE

Remember
the receiver

waiting
in its cradle

where an answer
could remain.

Recall
the rotary

where without
the ring

we could not
know

if the call
even was.

It was easier,
then, to lie

about
our absences.

How we could
pick up

with silence,
blame the line,

invisible
to our name,

called over
and over,

our mouths lost
to response.

How we
could lift it,

check
the dial tone,

a flatline
of sound

confirming
our here.

How if we held
through the beat—

pulse, pulse, pulse—
we could break

into the dead,
busy the signal.

How we answered
with expectation

a prayer of who
might be.

Hello? for all
those times

it wasn't you.
Or was.

How we
didn't want

the hang up,
pulling

the cord under
the threshold,

dragging it into
another room,

like a small throb
of desire,

wrapping
the spirals

around our wrists,
binding ourselves

to the other-end
voice, wired.

Or the way we
unplugged

it from
the jack

to stop
the insistence,

how it sat,
watching us,

keeping
its place,

a monument
on top of phone books,

the yellowed exchanges
of possibility.

And the way we
—almost—

effortlessly
left

it behind,
closing the door

on its persuasions,
never imagining

already it was
a parasite,

that we
were the ones

unable to be
left

to our own
devices.

MESSENGER

We talk to the ghost
surface, will a reply,

a buzz, a beacon,
anything to fend off

the dark we create.
Silence.

We leave you overturned.
Punished.

Slate of non-answers,
deprived of dopamine,

we cover you, come back
hours later, telling ourselves

Be someone
Be someone

We try again,
beg the center button.

Again.

No red numbers,
no alerts, only

time staring
back at us,

our sad
non-reflections

in the outrage
of our hands.

SELF SHOT

Selfish for what I cannot have,
I hold your sudden face in my hands,
persuade myself that I can keep you.

How cruel I am in my screen need,
the way I pin you to my want, whisper
to your photo shimmering over the surface

tension of my phone. Tensile suffocation:
how I bring you closer with the parting
of thumb and forefinger,

how I hone in on your eye that looks
to a lens, trick myself into believing
you are looking for me.

I will my body into your self shot,
the invitation of space next to you,
lying that it holds itself for us.

How quick I am to claim
regret as love. If this was love
I would unbuckle you.
But see, even there.

I am making you naked in the words,
stripping you versus saying
cut yourself away, run while you can.

EIFFEL TOWER: FIRST TIME

*after Gustave Eiffel: "Do not the laws of natural forces always
conform to the secret laws of harmony?"*

Twenty hours into the day and we land in Paris.
We run streets, stop for maps, turn ourselves
until we find it. At last, under the girders and lines

I spin, my arms out, all the years I have written
myself here converge. I release. My voice
sparks the air and its points: *Paris! Paris!*

My arms are a clock, broken from winding,
my numbers drop, unriveted for this moment
outside time. And I run to you. I want

you to lose me under this four-cornered
monument, this unreal iron dream made tangible,
to take my body and snap its boundaries

but you hold me without kissing back, tell me
not here, not now. And I shift myself into a pause
I do not want, wait to break our embrace.

We start to walk the gravel. I fall behind.
I stop and turn back, look up to the steeled shock,
the proclamation once temporary, now iconic.

When you see that I do not follow, you turn
to ask why. I say better to see the light.
My hands are a steeple beneath my chin.

Husband, do I will you to be who you cannot?
A man who kisses away the years we'd forgotten
in each other, a man whose lips press
the breath from me, whose intensity

is pointed heavenward, who collapses

with me on the grass and thinks nothing of other eyes,
only the drowning and baptism of our bodies?

I want you to make us
new again, as in our first kiss
from so long ago, my glass so full.

You return to stand quietly behind me.
You tell me we are older now.
Your hands find my waist.
I know you want to go.

But somehow
it all seems monumental.

Can I love you in this,
the way that you give?

Can I forgive
that there may never be more?

VOW

And in the rolling night,
drinks raised in laughter
and toast, there is the lure

of crepe, us winding ourselves,
tangled in green, swirling
down from the apex of dance.

We spin with each other, collapse
on the couch. You right
my glass, somehow still full.

Your hands meet as a cup.
My face fills them.
I realize I was wrong
about everything. Even you.

Your eyes study the rises
and corners of my cheeks.
You hold the moment before
the meeting. Because how

could we know this night
would sudden itself sacred?
When we pause, we open

our eyes to each other.
Your first impulse is to speak
my entire name. As if in calling.

You say I am a place
lifted from every geography.

Who wouldn't have said *yes*
to one who promised
a life of such discovery?

Who wouldn't have said
I do?

ON THE UNDERGROUND

Sated by London, we ride the Tube
back to Bank, you in your indigo
tie, my anniversary present
already loosening its knot.

Our children are an ocean away.
We are able to love our quiet love.
Content, you take my hand, sigh in to me.
We hold this gaze until I become sleepy,
turn to rest my head on your shoulder.

Eighteen years. I smile to myself.
Today we did not have to argue
over the bills. I did not have to pull
your socks from the bed. Again. We
even shared an orange. Across the way

I become distracted by her short black boots,
zippers traversing her ankle, glittering
tracks to her toes. Yes, I think, to have
those teeth. Golden too. I follow her body
to shadow stockings, leather skirt, higher

still to leopard scarf, raven bob,
the bright surprise of her lips, red
in the dark of these tunnels. Her ears,
beaded to headphones, unknown music.

Looking out the passing glass,
she glances down, sees our hands.
Her face registers, softens. She does not see

that I see. I watch how she loses her body,
her edges. I loosen my fingers, slide them
under my scarf. I know this look,
have given it too. She is making you hers.

Once, I would have pinned her in stare,
squeezed your hand in triumph, as if
I owned a thing. But I see this differently
now. Her eyes cast further into a certain light.

I close my own. Let her have you for as long
as she needs. Even if she leads you, nameless,
into her imaginary bed. For now you are her
greatest pleasure. In time she will remember
you as the man with the diamond

tie, the fantasy whose arched lips she unleashed
over her body. I cannot tell her these lips
are the same ones I daily curse, kiss, marry
again. Instead I want her to have you,

keep you, love this unknown love. Let her make
you this beautiful, this pure, your hand open
to hers, the rushing train, let her hold you
forever in it.

PASSING HUGO BOSS

And then there was the longing,
the sudden negative space, silent
as yearn, as filament wrapped
through me, and I pass a shirt,
a department store display, folded
perfectly, some fingers edging seams
over cardboard, laying it out crisp,
at angle, the white poplin, the small
blue stripes, his exact color of blue.
I know the designer before I see the name.

I know, in that sudden rush of charge
it is *the* shirt, the one he bought weeks ago,
in his transformation. I know
it irrevocably, my body speaking to me
in its thunder. Feel it now, how I am

walking past, in regular, expected space,
how in one glance they line up within me,
these pins, spines, rachis of feathers,
vibrating, oscillating, villi moving
with the charge of every bolt, and in the singe
from my brain to the fired marble behind
my pubic bone, the whole forest blazes,
contained under my skin.

I want to stop, to touch the shirt, but I never lose
my stride, or the fruit that breaks within me,
the splitting from seed, this pain swirled
into the color of pleasure, this ache that wraps down
into fist, protection, but also wide
in inflorescence, every last raging gem
shattering outward. Oh God, my God, it is why

we say it, because there is no way
to tell this, what do we call it: longing,

missing, yearning, there is no way for bodies
to take this noise and sharpness, implosion
and reckless breaking and bring it to word
or image. How did I know it was the shirt,
you will ask. Do you even need confirmation?

It was because my body knew it,
just as the feeling spiked in me every
time the moment before I ran into him, every hair
standing on toes, knowing the strike of lightning,
imminent. There was no swerving or stopping,
no hands held up in protection, only the swift
shot of voltage, the tingling heat left
in the bowl of my body, and me, still walking,

stepping forward, no one around me knowing
that I'd been touched, zapped, my body carrying
the joules of wavelength, this parallel, him wearing
this very poplin right now, on his first night out
since the divorce. And he is looking into the bottom

of his wine glass and he thinks, maybe, he sees
my face looking back from the surface,
and without conscious awareness, he reaches up,
touches the mole on his neck, the small circle
of darkness that I would kiss, saying:
this is my mark, my space on your body,

and this is where I will be no matter how he travels,
no matter what storm opens above, what fierce light
grabs us from the sky, fuses us, glass under the sand,
this fulgurite spreading, hidden under the beach for miles.

IT'S ALL REAL WITHIN THE DREAM

This is not monumental.
We are sitting next to each other
on the couch. Through the window
there is a sun. I am looking at your faded knee,
denim fibers worn to fine over your most bendable
places. We are holding hands. Everywhere,
somewhere, people are holding hands.
Even now in the poem, even as you read this,
even when you find these forgotten words
a lifetime later, we are holding hands. This
is not remarkable. Forget that you live
on one side of the world and I the other.
Forget that it has been seventeen years since
I have seen you. This is ordinary, your hand
in mine, me feeling a small pulse
from your wrist. We are sitting on a couch.
Together. There is the sun. This is not extraordinary.
We are looking to each other. I don't have to find you
across wires, photos, pixelated text.
There is the air of you. There is the air of me.
There is our air, together. We breathe. You,
tangible in my senses. Me, tangible in yours.
This is just a Tuesday. This is not remarkable.
You say: *When I look back over my life*
I will count this as one of my happiest moments.
Everywhere people are holding hands. Everywhere
there is a sun, even when we turn from it. See?
We are still holding hands. You have said
those words to me. Still we are sitting
on the couch. You are wearing jeans. There is us.
There were seventeen years. We feel our hands together.
We cannot stop looking. Everything is unremarkable.
Somewhere everyone is holding hands. The sun
wants to slip, to remind us. At last we can touch
each other. Don't wake me if it isn't true.

THE PERSISTENCE OF WANT

When we meet and I open
the book of us, there
must be an eye for fire:

all the things written before
the smallness of us: composed,
sexed, painted, bled into being,
talked into creation, like,

that at last, there is your pulse
wishing against me, your arms
taking me, the willingness
of geography closed. I write this

poem under every day, scenarios
scratched and crossed into existence,
destruction: how we leave and never
return, the restraint, the volatile,
the never meet, us both alone

in different countries, as it should be.
I turn my prized sphere of story for comfort,
tension, lust, nostalgia, to relive and invent
you in the words because here

you don't go, we keep each other, we
change the possible with every letter.

But what if, in the wounded reckless
skin of you, pressed to the wounded
reckless skin of me, there is the (un)lock?
In our imagined met: no more why
or what if, only the frayed

human shirt, your edge so close to my
eye, the vision made touch, and too

this will go into memory, interpretation,
story. But I only want this impossible

present, the space of us fissured in a space,
the nervous anticipatory ricochet of heart
so near to heart, the non-words bleeding
through us, our faulty thoughts, our errant
bodies, the commitments we hold and question.

There is only the implosion,
your face setting over mine, the relief
of prayer made flesh. We can break
the spell of water. We brought our bodies
together again. And our faces close distance,
time. And in the second before we seal this, kiss

that almost kiss, the tainted moment
where I want every button undone,
the swim of our bodies back, where you too
can think only of the fall of break,
the feel of us, on, in each other,

I want us both somehow
to do the inconceivable: to willingly
pull back, to choose to create
some altered love where all of these marriages

we have made keep us and we let them,
where even in our devastating bodies
we choose higher, we stay at embrace.

LETTER TO MY HUSBAND

Forgive me, husband.
I was bold enough to believe
I could vow my life, think that if I loved
my best, turned my ways, that the aching
story would leave us be.

I did not understand then the fault
of erosion, the determination
to move from would be the very sinking.
That those quiet nights when I listened
to the siren calls of memory,
the incantation of questions left open,
that I would always heed, not knowing
yet there was a choice.

And you freed me anyway, to unseam
the wound, to take its deepest pain
and lift it back to light, to at last admit.
Maybe I should not ask forgiveness.
This darkness in my eyes led you here,
made me. And you have never blamed
my tendency for distance, my foul habit
of seeking *what if* for fulfillment. Instead

you held me all along, your love
that never denied, even when my haunted hands
preferred the dark, my feet favored the splinter
of unsteady boards. You held me as I called
his name, rinsed him through me, polished
my stone of regret. And still, you loved

the fertile broken girl, even as she claimed him.
But look now. She has her story. The myth
continues to rise. She is no longer restless,
wandering the stairs of my heart
with her bitter candle. She is crawling

next to you, into our crisp,
scattered sheets, knowing
that because of love
she can at last wake to live.

THOU ART ALIVE STILL

Thou art alive still
While thy book doth live
And have wits to read
And praise to give

sign above the door, Shakespeare and Company Bookstore, Paris, France

July 9, 2012

I

In front of the sign, you unpocket
your hands, look to what they hold. Count
the grid beneath your feet—seventh stone
square from the door, third from the street.
The dream made tangible, at last the arrival
of your body. And now, the place of collide:
past, present, and as-yet condense,
become our kilometer zero.

The throb of red geraniums shock from the sill,
windows thrown open over the capitals:
SHAKESPEARE AND CO.
You raise your phone, seal the split second:
five lights burn through the pane, your profile
caught in the glass, the edge of evening
rubbing in from the Seine. Before sunset,

Paris is an accordion of light behind you.
On your screen the image hovers, captured.
You lower the phone—camera, carrier.
Palm turned to sky, you letter my name
into the blank, touch the word *send*.

II

Bed dense with afternoon, I roll
from slumber and into your Paris,

102

as if I had slipped into your body,
petal lifted from the bow, the apparition
of it all. Prayer of my palms. You in my hands.

The way I receive. How long did I hold
my breath, your photo, knowing you stood
just there, waiting for me to open? How long
did you remain on that stone, touching
my initials, willing the message to go through,
arrive as the buzz in my body?

What I cannot know: how you wished each gesture
a spell, the letters of my name an incantation
you could conjure, and I would appear,
the woman rising from the bench just now,
looking to you, then to the door,
eyes taking her anywhere.

July 19, 2012

III

Ten days later I wake on Rue Rampon and unpack
the green dress. I have not worn it before today,
this slip of a thing, just opaque, thin threads of gold
visible only when the eye is intimate. It shows my skin,
flirts with my knees, traces itself into my body.

From the quai I see it: 37 Rue de la Bûcherie.
The heat rush of faint tremors through me. I turn
to the water to breathe. Notre Dame calls from
the periphery. Somehow I find the altar, my knees.
Somehow the light chooses me.

I cleave to the bridge of my folded hands, undo
the harness of time. Words rise from my hips
to my mouth: *forgive me, forgive this*. They begin as whispers.
I imagine they are my silence, the warp and weft woven

through the danger of my ache, the wide open quarry
that spells all of our loss. But I am wrong.

I am loud enough to cut a hymn, loud enough
that another voice rises, shocks the air, sudden
in its English: *there is nothing to be forgiven!*
Invisible mouth, unknown alcove.
My words, his, colliding in the above:
A response? A coincidence? A pardon?

I allow my eyes the light, the flame wave
that hungers for it all: the years of shame and guilt,
the words, stained in their loneliness. The silence
that spoke too much. I watch as the wick
darkens itself to ash, as the scrim of wax
hardens to white. We have unsealed it all.

Under stone saints I rise, unleash the gallop
of my body, allow my mouth the only questions
I have left:

How can I love?
How can I not love?

Outside the doors I run, a train dividing the night,
my eyes open with intention, the stone square
no longer untouchable. A home. A call.
This time where I choose to stand.

IV

I take your photo from my pocket, place my feet
over the once feet of yours. I hold your version
to the sky, align us, our vision. *Ten days ago* repeats
like a benediction. The geranium leaves continue their curl
in parallel pattern, blooms not yet changed to my view
or yours. My eyes of split reality: this of what I hold,
this of what I see. The broken comes as thunder now:

Do you feel as I feel, the fracture of *ifs*, all the ways
we chose not to be? The window pales in the sky shift
of storm, glass holding then releasing: mirage of merged
bodies, past, the city of us reaching in from the angles.

In my photo there will be five burning lamplights,
emerald in their lure. At the end of the dock I see them,
boy and girl, painted into the sign. How they hold hands.
How they open for the words. How their eyes
were always facing ours, as if anticipating embrace.

I raise my camera to seal it all, knowing I can never
capture a thing, the knock of my entire body as I slide
to unlock, as I swipe over the icon that takes, as I lower
myself to the ground, right there on our stone in Paris,
this pool of green, this photo made, the ghosts of us merged
and nowhere near, the first place we share in over twenty years,
just as with our stone square in Toledo, dreaming Monet.

CÔTE D'AZUR, SEVENTEEN YEARS LATER

after Claude Monet's Antibes Seen from La Salis, *Toledo Museum of Art*

It begins in gold, this pointing
upward of leaves. How the branches
rise, propose an unseen union.

Note the olive tree, the hidden
live in its name, the way it arrives,
mouthed, silent, as *I love*.

Wonder about the couple, left unpainted,
how we imagined ourselves
then, stippled as a tangle in the grass,

kept from Monet's canvas. How we held
this vision in our years of absence: the tinge
of me inseparable from the mark of you.

What Monet said of this place: it was impossible
to paint without gemstones, its beautiful madness
a fairy tale of air and light.

Listen to the dazzle of that waiting city,
the way it calls us to believe. How we want
to dismiss the story, drown innocence

in the sea below. After seventeen years, a quarry
of space between us, I return to this landscape.
I open my hand to a fairy tale of air and light—

expect only memory, not the sudden slide
of your fingers, taking mine, or how we paint
ourselves here, again, into the impossible.

SLIDE TO UNLOCK: BLUE NOTE

July 19, 2012

In my pocket I carry a painting.
The violets and golds press their heat

against memory, skin. The card, blank
for this moment, holds only a landscape:

Antibes Seen from La Salis.
Our Monet of Toledo, taken to Paris,

from our tandem stone, to another stone:
seventh from the door, third from the street.

I rise under the falling light, the words
untethering the undertow of our bodies,

salt of our silence. The letters, read, spoken.
The words we walk under and through:

Shakespeare and Company Antiquarian Books.
The door is an invitation, the threshold,

a release. Us: two who sought synchronicity,
unsecreted salvation, freed silence

from the lock of time. To come alive in the tension
of possibility: our call. Our calling,

at last, answered. Or begun.
I leave the words: *betrayal, infidelity.*

I leave the years of apology, the nights
my empty hands sought the air for you,

resolution. I find the blue chair.
I will not remember what I wrote,

only that I thanked you for all the years,
your way of loving, honoring our storied ways.

Part of me could feel you assemble beside me,
sense your hand in my words after all of this time.

My virgin love. Muse. Fantasy of wires.
Our glass city. I seal this all between the pages.

Behind the iron gates of the poetry shelves
I leave you

an envelope, never knowing if the planet
will permit, spin in such a way that you find it.

July 12, 2013

You text me a picture: the tufted blue chair.
My God, you are in Paris. It is the chair

where I wrote you: the one broken
beneath the seat, hollowed to sit.

Hallowed too. But you know this already.
Your next photo: the letter, propped against

Margaret Atwood, just as I left it a year
before. The wrecked girl of me is holding

you near the water, our last place. We never went back.
This you know too. There were other ways, you'd said,

and this was one. Of course you read
my words in our chair. Of course you know

what I will ask before I ask it. You find our stone
square, place your feet over the once feet of mine.

And in this we meet again.
You hold the envelope, photograph

your name in my writing, the bookstore behind.
All these shifts of reflection, return.

I have never told you about *Before Sunset*, that open
end. Always this is how I see us: that precipice

of possible. It makes no sense. I am betrothed
to another life. Yet the ring is not a lock.

Some things in me cannot be held.
I married a man that knew this and somehow

blessed my brokenness: always part of me
is you. And he loves me still.

Sometimes I think it is true of us all. That those
loves that build and break us

are always our loves to be wreathed
in odd gratitude, to be released to roam

in our recesses. Not to be clutched,
prisoned in a bent photograph, sullied

in a drawer of regret. We led them
to those they love now. We dance over

so many boundaries, question them all.
Part of me will always lament that I cannot open

my body to you, my body that first learned
to open because of you. But the call is to love

in ways beyond the cell, and in this, there is more:
words, art, the danger of our electric phones.

You photograph the letter in your hands now.
I am as with you as I ever will be. We are still our book,

writing. You walk to the café next door, order
a glass of soave. You text me a toast: *We are here*

you type, *our energy, the ways we love in this life,*
the ways we love story. Go, lift the words, our book,

into the truth. It was never ours. I will be waiting.
And what you don't tell me is this:

I've left you a letter. It is written on blue paper.
This one we will open together, our covers

joined, the spine of us bent to half circle,
releasing all of the loves who could not

love. Watch how they break
the surface, how they begin

their words.
Admit their story too.

NOTES

"Letters on the Air (I Feel Love)": italicized lyrics are from "I Feel Love," "Heaven Knows," "On the Radio," "Try Me I Know We Can Make It," "Last Dance," and "MacArthur Park."

"Bodies of Water: Discovering Côte d'Azur on Bird Lake" references *Ophelia ("And He Will Not Come Back Again")*, c. 1865, Arthur Hughes, Toledo Museum of Art. This is the only known Pre-Raphaelite painting where Ophelia turns from the water to make direct eye contact before her death. The phrase "town turned gold by the sun" is from Monet's letters, specifically: "I'm painting…Antibes, a small fortified town turned gold by the sun, standing out against beautiful blue and pink mountains and the everlastingly snow covered Alps."

"Lock Bridge, 2008": from 2008 until 2015 couples attached padlocks to Pont des Arts in Paris as a declaration of love. The weight of the locks—over 45 tons in 2015—caused the collapse of bridge panels and ultimately led to their removal. In 2014, the "Love Without Locks" campaign discouraged the practice with the reminder: "Our bridges can no longer withstand your gestures of love."

"It's All Real Within the Dream" references a recollection shared by Ward Briggs during James Dickey's memorial service, January 27, 1997: "(Jim) told me he had a dream…he was back in high school playing football and he had scored the first touchdown, and then he scored the second touchdown. He was carried off the field and that night went to a party where the most beautiful girl in all the state of Georgia fell in love with him. They ended the evening by the side of a country road with the top down and moonlight showering them. He said to her, 'This is the greatest day of my life, but I can't be happy.' She said, 'Why not?' and he said, 'This is just a dream; it's not real.' She said, 'Sure it's real, Jim. It's all real within the dream.' He asked me when the end came…to tell him… 'It's all real, Jim, in the dream,' and I promised I would. A little more than a week ago, I was in his room and I grabbed his hand at the end of our conversation, and I said, 'Just remember, Jim, it's all real in the dream.' And he said, 'I know it is,' and he squeezed my hand."

"Côte d'Azur, Seventeen Years Later" refers to both Monet's 1888 letter to his companion, Alice Hoschedé, regarding Antibes — "What I will bring back from here will be pure, gentle sweetness: some white, some pink, and some blue, and all this surrounded by the fairytale-like air"—and to his 1888 letter to Rodin: "I am fencing and wrestling with the sun. And what a sun it is! In order to paint here one would need gold and precious stones."

ACKNOWLEDGMENTS

I wish to thank the editors of the following journals and publications in which these poems first appeared:

Bridge Eight: "Electric Mail"
Chautauqua Literary Journal: "Blood"
A Constellation of Kisses: "Eiffel Tower: First Time" (Terrapin Press)
Cortland Review: "Letters on the Air (I Feel Love)," "It's All Real Within the Dream"
Crab Orchard Review: "Pulse Storm, 2008"
Drunken Boat: "Switching Off at Cedar Point"
Ekphrastic Review: "Slide to Unlock: Blue Note"
Escape Into Life: "Vow," "Self Shot," "Seeing an Ex on the Beach"
Fall Lines: "Infidelity," "The Call"
Four Chambers: "Venice"
Gulf Coast: "Observations From the Base"
James Dickey Review: "The Hang Up," "Telephone, Call"
Muse/A Journal: "Finger Sequence in Blue"
Nasty Women Poets: An Unapologetic Anthology of Subversive Verse: "Scar Season" (Lost Horse Press)
Palooka: "Composition," "Gospel of Text, Books I-IV," "Email from Museo Correr," "On the Underground," "The Persistence of Want"
Pine Hills Review: "You're Breaking Up," "Foreign Exchange," "Passing Hugo Boss"
Poet Lore: "Darkroom"
Prairie Schooner: "Seventeen," "Glass City"
The Raven Chronicles: "Touch Tone: Random Access Memory"
South Dakota Review: "Lock Bridge, 2008," "Bodies of Water: Discovering Côte d'Azur on Bird Lake"
Toledo Museum of Art, Ekphrastic Series: "Côte d'Azur, Seventeen Years Later"
White Stag Journal: "Severed," "Statue Prayer at Fifteen"

"Infidelity" was a finalist for the 2016 Saluda River Poetry Prize.

"Côte d'Azur, Seventeen Years Later" was the winning poem for the 2015 Toledo Museum of Art Ekphrastic Poetry Prize.

"Electric Mail" was a finalist for the 2014 Pirate's Alley Faulkner Society Words and Music Award.

"Glass City" is written with gratitude, love, and holy intention for my hometown.

"Letters on the Air (I Feel Love)" is for Donna Summer, whose voice ignited my love of language.

"It's All Real Within the Dream" is for my ever archer who ever believed, James Dickey.

"Letter to My Husband" is for Mark, who willingly chose to love an artist all of those years ago, knowing even then that part of me would always be rooted in memory, story, and poetry. And who continues to embrace me as family despite it all.

"Côte d'Azur, Seventeen Years Later" is for the Toledo Museum of Art and its founders, Edward Drummond and Florence Scott Libbey.

"Slide to Unlock: Blue Note" (written in honor of Richard Linklater, Julie Delpy, and Ethan Hawke) manifested from an intentional and reverent act of kindness on which this book was created.

My gratitude to all of those that believed in *Slide to Unlock*. Your love is present here.

Profound thanks to fellow Toledo loves who renewed my faith and held the light: Sarah Taylor Myers and Matthew Dean Wilder. And for Jeff Pierce, a better angel, whose all-too-brief life lit the bonfire that meant I had to write this book. I hope I was brave enough.

For Gareth and Phoebe, who generously and lovingly shared their mother so this book could come to be. And to those that helped love this book into the world: my Payne, Huntsbarger, Bloemeke, and O'Neill families, and to the Raymond family, who are family.

To my teachers that guided me, even in the interims and sometimes without knowing, I have boundless thanks: James Dickey, April Bernard, Don Greiner, Janet Sylvester, Ed Madden, Larry Grimes, and Lana Hartman Landon. And to Jane Hirshfield, whose love, kindness, companioning, and belief nurtured my persistence.

To those who read this manuscript with a jeweler's eye and were generous with huzzah and tough love: Beth Gylys, Bella Pollen, Brent Calderwood, Wyn Cooper, Amanda Auchter , Sandra Beasley, Jericho Brown, Kelly Cockerham, Collin Kelly, Amy Pence, Alice Friman, and William Wright.

To my Toledo public school teachers who named me writer long before I could see, and who selflessly and enthusiastically believed: Judy Racicot, Ellen Gibney, Verdis Fields, Catherine Greebe, and Judy Slane. To St. Ursula Academy and the visionary that was Sister Mary Rose Krupp. I am ever your marigold. And to Bethany College, American University, University of South Carolina, and Bennington College.

With profound gratitude to and for the Virginia Center for the Creative Arts and Elizabeth Coles Langhorne. And with love for Jaquira Díaz, Howie Axelrod, Mario Danneels, and my fellow angel badass, Bella Pollen.

My gratitude to the Bowers family, Laura Bowers Foreman, Ellen Davenport, and to the haven of the Bowers House for solace and time to create.

To Julie and the Wenig family for offering time at the beloved cottage to write, create, and revise. That so many of these poems came into their own at Bird Lake, on my grandmother's table, is both a gift and a miracle made possible only by their benevolence for and trust in a complete stranger.

Rockstar gratitude and love for Collin Kelley whose consistent commitment and enthusiasm for this manuscript was a brilliant light.

To Bryan Borland, Seth Pennington, and Sibling Rivalry Press for seeing the vision, for our shared love of synchronicity, and for their adamant commitment to connection between poems, art, poets and readers.

With cosmos encompassing love for Kelly Cockerham, ever my sister in poetry, and Amy Gopp, ever my sister in soul.

For God and the undaunting love and healing of Magnetic Springs, Ohio. And for the Disciples of Christ church, where I learned that words were meant to have magic and freedom in interpretation, and that faith was about the questions, not the answers.

For M, who reminds me that we are never alone in the memory. And who meets me in the water every last time.

And, most especially, for my muse, who was, is, and ever shall be sealed in our envelope in Paris.

ABOUT THE POET

Julie E. Bloemeke is a native of Toledo, Ohio. She received an MFA through the Bennington Writing Seminars, and an MA from the University of South Carolina, where she was chosen as a Ramsaur Fellow and studied with James Dickey. Currently in Atlanta, Georgia, she has served as a fellow at the Virginia Center for the Creative Arts and has also been in residency at the Bowers House Literary Center. Her poems have been widely anthologized and appeared in numerous literary journals including *Gulf Coast, Prairie Schooner, Poet Lore, Chautauqua Literary Journal, Palooka Magazine, South Dakota Review, The Cortland Review, Bridge Eight Literary Magazine*, and others. Her ekphrastic work has been published and showcased in collaborations with the Toledo Museum of Art and Phoenix Museum of Art. A freelance writer, editor, and guest lecturer, her interviews have recently appeared in *The AWP Writer's Chronicle* and in *Poetry International*. *Slide to Unlock* was a finalist and semi-finalist for multiple book prizes including the May Swenson Poetry Prize in 2016. It is her first full-length poetry collection.

ABOUT THE PRESS

Sibling Rivalry Press is Sibling Rivalry Press is an independent press based in Little Rock, Arkansas. It is a sponsored project of Fractured Atlas, a nonprofit arts service organization. Contributions to support the operations of Sibling Rivalry Press are tax-deductible to the extent permitted by law, and your donations will directly assist in the publication of work that disturbs and enraptures. To contribute to the publication of more books like this one, please visit our website and click *donate*.

Sibling Rivalry Press gratefully acknowledges the following donors, without whom this book would not be possible:

Anonymous (18)	Andrea Lawlor
Arkansas Arts Council	Anthony Lioi
John Bateman	Ed Madden & Bert Easter
W. Stephen Breedlove	Mitchell, Blackstock, Ivers & Sneddon, PLLC
Dustin Brookshire	Stephen Mitchell
Sarah Browning	National Endowment for the Arts
Billy Butler	Stacy Pendergrast
Asher Carter	Simon Randall
Don Cellini	Paul Romero
Nicole Connolly	Randi M. Romo
Jim Cory	Carol Rosenfeld
Risa Denenberg	Joseph Ross
John Gaudin	In Memory of Bill Rous
In Memory of Karen Hayes	Matthew Siegel
Gustavo Hernandez	Alana Smoot
Amy Holman	Katherine Sullivan
Jessica Jacobs & Nickole Brown	Tony Taylor
Paige James	Leslie Taylor
Nahal Suzanne Jamir	Hugh Tipping
Allison Joseph	Guy Traiber
Collin Kelley	Mark Ward
Trevor Ketner	Robert Wright

CPSIA information can be obtained
at www.ICGtesting.com
Printed in the USA
LVHW011209010320
648601LV00004B/1373

9 781943 977765